Sunset Park

by Marley Sims
& Elliot Shoenman

A SAMUEL FRENCH ACTING EDITION

SAMUEL FRENCH

FOUNDED 1830

NEW YORK HOLLYWOOD LONDON TORONTO

SAMUELFRENCH.COM

ISBN 978-0-573-69603-9   Printed in U.S.A.   #20729

IMPORTANT BILLING AND CREDIT
REQUIREMENTS

SUNSET PARK premiered at the Zephyr Theatre in Los Angeles, California on April 28, 2005. The production was Directed by Mark L. Taylor and Produced by Daniel Shoenman, with the following cast:

EVELYN . . . . Sheila Oaks
ROSE . . . . Jennie Ventriss
CAROL . . . . Melanie Chartoff
ROGER . . . . Jim Ortlieb
YOUNG EVELYN . . . . Salli Saffioti
BENNY . . . . Aaron Jettleson
ABE . . . . Murray Rubin

Set & Lighting Design by Nathan Matheny
Sound Design by David McGuire
Costume Design by Valerie Laven-Cooper
Stage Manager - Kim Crabtree

SUNSET PARK re-opened at the Zephyr Theatre, Los Angeles, California on October 14, 2005. The production was Directed by Mark L. Taylor and Produced by Daniel Shoenman, with the following cast:

EVELYN . . . . Sheila Oaks, Jennie Ventriss
ROSE . . . . Jo Deotato Clark, Pat Crawford Brown
CAROL . . . . Melanie Chartoff, Rhonda Aldrich
ROGER . . . . Jim Ortlieb, Michael Mantel
YOUNG EVELYN . . . . Salli Saffioti, Stacy Keanan
BENNY . . . . Aaron Jettleson, Jason Field
ABE . . . . Murray Rubin, Stu Nisbet

Set & Lighting Design by Nathan Matheny
Sound Design by David McGuire
Costume Design by Valerie Laven-Cooper
Stage Manager - Kim Crabtree

CHARACTERS

EVELYN – mid-70's, widowed, acerbic, reasonably healthy.

ROSE – mid-70's, widowed, down-to-earth, in failing health.

CAROL – 50-ish, a single mother, high strung and neurotic.

ROGER – late 40' s, married, children, ambitious yet practical.

YOUNG EVELYN – mid-20's, pregnant.

BENNY – mid-20's, blue collar, full of dreams.

ABE – late 70's, broken down, grumpy and demanding.

ACT ONE

Scene One

(*A homey kitchen in a Brooklyn pre-war building.* **EVELYN
HOROWITZ,** *mid-seventies, has resided here for fifty years and
it's clear that this is the most lived-in room in the apartment.
An old Formica table and four chairs are center stage. An
upright piano is against the wall.*)

(**EVELYN** *and her best friend,* **ROSE IPPILITO,** *in her late sev-
enties, are at the table reading the Sunday New York Times
and having coffee.*)

ROSE. According to the Doppler radar, it's going to be
eighteen degrees tomorrow, with a windchill factor of
minus three.

EVELYN. You can keep your Doppler and your radar. When
I want to know the weather, I like the old system: I
open the window and stick my head out. You want
more coffee?

ROSE. Only if you're having.

EVELYN. Rose, we go through this every time. If you want
more coffee, but I don't feel like having more coffee,
you won't have more coffee?

ROSE. I'm just being polite. After all, I am a guest in your
home.

EVELYN. You live across the hall. You're here fourteen times
a day. If you want more coffee, ask for more coffee.

ROSE. All right. Give me half a cup.

(**EVELYN** *shakes her head and pours* **ROSE** *a little coffee.
She then fills up her own cup. Both women fall into
an easy rhythm of sharing cream and sugar and then
resume reading the paper.* **EVELYN** *turns to the back of
the main section.*)

EVELYN. My God, look at this.

> (**ROSE** *moves her chair next to* **EVELYN** *and they read the obituaries together.*)

ROSE. *(crossing herself)* Jesus, Mary and Joseph. So many names this week. Did you ever notice how many people pass away right after New Year's?

EVELYN. It makes sense. The holidays are over, family goes back home, people get depressed; and if they're hanging on by a thread – Oh, no. Look who died. Lillian Brunswick.

ROSE. What a shame. Do we know her?

EVELYN. We know of her. She was the head of the Consumer Affairs Commission.

ROSE. I thought that was Bess Meyerson.

EVELYN. After her. Or maybe before. She was the first Jewish Miss America.

ROSE. Lillian Brunswick?

EVELYN. Bess Meyerson.

ROSE. How old was she? Lillian Brunswick.

EVELYN. *(reading obituary)* Eighty-six. 'After a prolonged battle with cancer.' Horrible. To have to suffer like that.

ROSE. Well, may she rest in peace. She's gone to a better place.

EVELYN. A hole in the ground.

ROSE. I know that's what you believe. But the idea that when you die that's it...I couldn't have gone on after losing Sal, if I didn't think that one day we'd be together again. Faith gives you strength. Especially when you get older.

EVELYN. For me it's the opposite. The older I get, the more I see, the less faith I have.

ROSE. You can't go by what you see.

EVELYN. What I see is all I have.

ROSE. And that's your problem, Evelyn. Maybe if you open up your mind, just a little, God could slip in there.

EVELYN. I've lived in this building for fifty years. I never even changed apartments. If God was looking for me, he could have found me.

ROSE. He's not supposed to find you, you're supposed find him.

EVELYN. Whatever the protocol, to me, you're born, you live, you die, with no help from a higher power. I live a very unencumbered existence. No one to thank, no one to blame.

ROSE. And nobody to look to when you're searching for comfort.

EVELYN. I can't look to somebody who I don't believe exists. Enough already. How many times do we have to have the same –

ROSE. All right, all right. You know me, I'm not one to push. You'll never hear it from me again.

EVELYN. *(under her breath)* Until tomorrow.

ROSE. You shouldn't do that.

EVELYN. What?

ROSE. Mumble insults under your breath. You used to pull your hair out when your father-in-law did it to you.

(This stops **EVELYN.***)*

EVELYN. You're right. I'm sorry...

(then)

Next time, I'll say it out loud.

ROSE. That would be better.

(The doorbell rings and **EVELYN** *crosses to it.)*

EVELYN. Who is it?

CAROL *(V.O.)* Ma, it's me.

*(***EVELYN** *opens the door and lets in her fifty year-old daughter,* **CAROL.***)*

EVELYN. What happened to your key?

CAROL. I forgot to bring it.

EVELYN. Why don't you just keep it on your key chain?

CAROL. Because I don't need it every day.

EVELYN. And the weight of it hurts your back?

CAROL. Nice to see you, too.

>   (CAROL *kisses* EVELYN, *then* ROSE.)

CAROL. Hi, Rose, how are you?

ROSE. I can't complain.

CAROL. That's where you and I part company. You look nice. What's different?

ROSE. *(indicating her hair)* I got layered.

EVELYN. And they say women our age have no sex drive.

ROSE. I said, 'layered.' Your hearing's going.

EVELYN. My hearing's fine. I was kidding.

CAROL. So, Rose, what's new with Connie?

ROSE. She's busy, between her work and the twins looking at colleges.

EVELYN. One wants to come here, to NYU.

ROSE. The other wants to stay in Los Angeles. What's your Lisa thinking about?

CAROL. Usually, boys.

EVELYN. What are you saying? She's a very good student. Straight A's. And a very talented actress. She could have her pick of colleges.

CAROL. But she'll probably stay local.

ROSE. Keep them close. That's what I say. Because once they leave, good luck. Well, I should get going. I have to put my feet up.

EVELYN. Your ankles?

ROSE. I could hardly get my shoes on this morning.

EVELYN. What'd you eat last night?

ROSE. Nothing different. I'm very careful.

>   *(to* CAROL*)*

> Used to be I could eat everything; now I have to scrape the salt off a Ritz cracker…

>   *(to* EVELYN*)*

> What do you want me to leave you?

EVELYN. Let me have the Book Review and Travel.

(ROSE *separates the paper.*)

ROSE. Good to see you, Carol. Say hello to Lisa for me.

CAROL. Will do. And send my love to Connie and her family.

(ROSE *exits with the rest of the paper.*)

EVELYN. You want lox and bagels? I bought fresh.

CAROL. Nah. I'm watching my carbs. The last guy I went out with thought I was a little bottom heavy.

EVELYN. He told you that?

CAROL. Believe it or not, yes.

EVELYN. What do you need a jerk like that?

CAROL. In my situation, I'm lucky I can get a jerk.

EVELYN. What's wrong with your situation? You're smart, you're attractive –

CAROL. I'm fifty, menopausal, I've got bills out my ass…

EVELYN. Why won't you let me help you out a little?

CAROL. With what? You haven't got that much yourself.

EVELYN. I'm fine.

CAROL. I'm not taking your money, Ma.

(CAROL *crosses to the bathroom. As soon as she's gone,* EVELYN *takes a twenty dollar bill from her purse and slips it into* CAROL*'s purse. As* EVELYN *closes* CAROL*'s purse, the front door is opened with a key.* ROGER, *late forties, enters. He is dressed in casual but expensive clothing.*)

ROGER. Hi, Mom.

EVELYN. What are you doing here?

ROGER. It's Sunday. Remember, Carol and I take turns coming to visit. She comes one Sunday, I come the next.

EVELYN. Don't talk to me like I'm an idiot. I know the routine. And this is not your Sunday. It's Carol's Sunday.

ROGER. We switched. Carol's coming next Sunday instead of this Sunday.

EVELYN. That's going to be news to her.

    (CAROL enters.)

CAROL. What are you doing here?

ROGER. We switched. I told you, I'm going to the Giants' game and it was easier for me to get my visit to Mom in on the way, rather than make a separate trip next Sunday.

CAROL. We talked about that, but you never called to confirm it.

ROGER. Yes, I did. My secretary left a message at your office.

CAROL. Oh, did she? Well, my secretary…Wait a minute, I am the secretary. I never got a message or I wouldn't be here today. I've got a million other things I could be doing.

ROGER. So go do them. I'm here.

CAROL. I'm here, too. Why should I be the one who leaves and has to schlep myself back here next week?

ROGER. Because my schlep is twice as long as yours.

CAROL. Oh, poor you. Dragging yourself in from Long Island in your brand new Mercedes, while I'm riding the goddamn subway which runs every twenty minutes on the weekend.

EVELYN. I can't tell you how heartwarming it is to see my children fight over me this way…I'll tell you what, why don't you both do me a favor and go home?

CAROL. Ma…

ROGER. It's not a big deal.

CAROL. We didn't mean it the way it sounded.

ROGER. We'll work it out.

EVELYN. I don't need you to work anything out. And I don't need you to come here every week and check up on me. I'm healthy as a horse.

CAROL. A horse with a heart condition.

EVELYN. They never proved it was a heart condition.

CAROL. You passed out on the train.

EVELYN. It was hot.

ROGER. It was January. Dr. Goldstein said you had an irregular heartbeat.

EVELYN. I listen to him like I listen to the wall.

ROGER. If you don't think he's any good, why have you been going to him forever?

EVELYN. He's the best of the worst. Meanwhile, it's been three years and I haven't had any problems since. You want to know what kind of shape I'm in? I subbed thirty hours this week. In kindergarten. That could kill a person half my age. Roger, you want a bagel and lox?

ROGER. No. I'm going to have something at the game.

CAROL. *(to* **EVELYN***)* Are you aware there are people your age who slow down a little?

EVELYN. On their way to the grave. I like teaching. It keeps me young.

*(*EVELYN *notices something on the table.)*

EVELYN. Look at this, Rose left her reading glasses again. If it wasn't for me, she'd spend half her life at Lenscrafters. I'll be right back.

*(*EVELYN *takes the glasses and starts for the door.)*

CAROL. Walk slow.

EVELYN. Yeah, yeah, yeah.

*(*EVELYN *exits.)*

CAROL. God, she's so stubborn. She drives me crazy.

ROGER. She's impossible. But look at the bright side, at least she's active. She's not sitting home all day, shuffling around in a housecoat.

CAROL. I think she's depressed.

ROGER. You think everybody's depressed.

CAROL. No, I don't. What I'm saying is, why do you think she's always out running around? So she doesn't have to sit by herself. I mean what does she have here? She's got one friend left in the building, we see her once a week. You know, the number one cause of depression in old people is loneliness.

ROGER. That's why I think it's good that she's out in the world doing things. Maybe she'll meet somebody.

CAROL. Who's she going to meet? All the men her age are dead.

ROGER. I'm not saying there's thousands, but there must be some men out there, widowers, who can still string a sentence together.

CAROL. Roger, Daddy's been dead for forty years. And in all that time, how many men would you say Mom dated?

ROGER. I don't know. Half a dozen maybe?

CAROL. And eventually she said the same thing about each and every one of them, 'He can't hold a candle to your father.'

ROGER. I don't get it. You know how much I love my wife, but if Allison died tomorrow, I'd certainly want to move on and hook up with somebody else. I mean, who wants to spend the rest of their life alone? Look what's it's already doing to you.

CAROL. Excuse me?

ROGER. I'm just saying you've gotten a little…bitter.

CAROL. I don't fucking believe you. First of all, my husband didn't die, although I wish he would have. He left me broke, hardly sees his daughter and may possibly be the biggest asshole on the planet. Thank you very much. This is just what I needed, to talk about Ira.

*(**CAROL** crosses to the refrigerator and opens it.)*

CAROL. Jesus Christ.

ROGER. What is it?

CAROL. Cheesecake. She's got a gigantic piece of cheese-cake in here.

(She takes it out of the refrigerator.)

CAROL. She's supposed to be watching her cholesterol, not eating this crap.

*(**CAROL** tastes the cheesecake with her finger.)*

CAROL. Oh, my God. This is incredible. Here taste.

(She offers him a finger full of cheesecake.)

ROGER. I'll get my own.

(**ROGER** *opens up a drawer and takes out a fork.*)

CAROL. Bring me one of those. And a knife.

(**ROGER** *obeys and they sit at the table and share the cheesecake.*)

CAROL. Do you know how much fat has got to be in here? This is the worst possible thing she could put in her body.

ROGER. It's like shooting cement into her arteries. Does she have any milk in there?

CAROL. I'll see.

(*As* **CAROL** *goes to the refrigerator, takes out a carton of milk and pours it into two large glasses,* **ROGER** *peruses a pile of mail on the table. A letter catches his eye.*)

ROGER. Holy shit. Look at this.

CAROL. What?

ROGER. The building's going co-op.

CAROL. You're kidding?

(**CAROL** *crosses to the table with the milk, sits and looks at the letter.*)

CAROL. I don't believe it. Two hundred and fifty thousands dollars for this place?

(**EVELYN** *enters to see her children eating her dessert.*)

EVELYN. What are you doing? That's my cheesecake.

CAROL. You're not supposed to eat stuff like this.

ROGER. (*holding up the letter*) Why didn't you tell us this place was going co-op?

EVELYN. What the hell is this? I leave for five minutes, the next thing I know, you're searching the premises and I'm under investigation. Would you like to frisk me, maybe I'm hiding a salami in my brassiere?

CAROL. Don't get so defensive, Ma.

ROGER. You left the letter sitting right here on the table. This is the second notice, the deadline to buy is Wednesday. When were you going to tell me?

EVELYN. Never. What is it your business?

ROGER. You don't understand.

CAROL. What does this mean? If she doesn't buy she has to move?

EVELYN. I'm not moving anywhere. I checked when the first notice came. The law says they have to offer the apartment to me, but I don't have to buy. My old lease is good for as long as I want it to be.

ROGER. Neither one of you is getting this. This is a huge opportunity. If you buy this apartment today for two fifty, you could turn around and sell it tomorrow for, probably, three and a quarter. Because you're already a tenant, they have to offer it to you at the low end of market value.

EVELYN. That's terrific. Except I don't have two hundred fifty thousand dollars and, even if I did, I'm not selling. This is my home.

ROGER. I'm not saying you should sell right away. I'm saying that this is a tremendous investment that'll pay off one day.

EVELYN. Meanwhile, I'll have all of the benefits of a co-op without putting up a nickel. They're fixing the lobby, putting in a new elevator, an intercom. I get all that for free while everybody else is paying an arm and a leg.

ROGER. Mom, you've been shelling out rent for fifty years. You won't have to do that anymore.

EVELYN. You're right. I don't know what I was thinking. First thing tomorrow, I'll put on my best bandana, march into the bank and hold it up.

ROGER. I'll put up the money.

EVELYN. You? You have that kind of money lying around?

ROGER. Let's just say, I have no problem putting up the down payment. And I'll take out a loan for the rest.

CAROL. That's fantastic. We're going to make a killing.

ROGER. Excuse me. Did you say, 'we'?

CAROL. Yeah. We're going to share the profits…right?

ROGER. Not right. If I'm making loan payments and taking all the risk, why should you get any of the benefits?

CAROL. What risk? I thought you said it was a sure thing.

ROGER. It is.

CAROL. Then why should you be the only one who makes money?

ROGER. That's the way it works. He who puts up the money, makes the money.

CAROL. So, I'm cut out of the whole deal?

ROGER. I'll say it slower. He who puts up the money, makes the money.

CAROL. You are such a putz.

EVELYN. Please, the two of you. Stop it. Roger, are you positive this apartment is worth more than what they're asking?

ROGER. Absolutely. This neighborhood is taking off. You saw what happened in Park Slope, even Williamsburg.

EVELYN. And this will be like that?

ROGER. Yeah. It's a trend. They're gentrifying the hell out of Brooklyn.

EVELYN. If that's really the case, then buying makes sense. But I want half the profits to go to Carol.

CAROL. Ah hah.

(to **ROGER***)*

Well, there you have it.

ROGER. *(to* **EVELYN***)* Why are you taking her side?

EVELYN. I'm not taking anybody's side. It's always bothered me that I have so little to leave the two of you. This way there'll be an inheritance.

ROGER. Which I would be financing. If she's going to get half, then she should put up half.

CAROL. Fine. If you're going to be that way, I'll take out my own loan.

ROGER. With your credit?

EVELYN. *(to* **CAROL***)* If I'm not going to be paying rent anymore, I could give that money to you and you can use it toward your half.

CAROL. Your rent money wouldn't make a dent in what I need. Besides, with that extra cash, you could treat yourself a little. And you could stop buying your Lipitor in Canada.

ROGER. You're getting your medication from Canada?

EVELYN. It's cheaper. The co-payment on my insurance went up.

ROGER. Why didn't you tell me? I would have helped you out.

EVELYN. I'm not taking your money.

CAROL. All right. How about this for a solution?

(to ROGER*)*

You lend me my half of the money and when we eventually sell, I'll pay you back.

EVELYN. That makes sense.

ROGER. No, it doesn't. It's bullshit.

(to EVELYN*)*

Because I have money and she doesn't, I get penalized?

EVELYN. You're not being penalized. It's a question of being fair. She's your sister.

ROGER. A sister who takes every opportunity to make nasty remarks about my car, my house…She resents my success until she needs something.

CAROL. Oh, please. Your big success was marrying a woman with money who had a father who made you a vice president of his company.

ROGER. Up yours.

CAROL. Up yours.

EVELYN. Stop it, both of you.

(ROGER *gets up and starts for the door.)*

ROGER. You know what, I don't need this. The hell with it.

(to CAROL*)*

And the hell with you.

EVELYN. Roger, calm down.

ROGER. I'm out of here.

CAROL. Good riddance.

ROGER. Fuck you.

CAROL. Fuck you.

(ROGER *exits slamming the door behind him.*)

EVELYN. What did you have to start with him for?

CAROL. Me? He's the one that started it. You said it yourself. He's a greedy bastard.

EVELYN. I never said that.

CAROL. I'm entitled to half the money.

EVELYN. I was trying to find a way to leave you something. But instead of letting me work it out, you had to start an argument with him.

CAROL. So now you're on his side?

EVELYN. You sound like you're nine years old. I'm not on anybody's side. You're both my children and you're both a pain in the ass.

Scene Two

(The stage is dark. We hear a cell phone conversation between CAROL *and* ROGER. *Their connection is poor and we hear a lot of background noise coming through their phones.)*

CAROL. Hello? Hello?

ROGER. It's Roger.

CAROL. I don't want to talk to you.

ROGER. What?

CAROL. I said, I don't want to talk to you.

ROGER. I'm sorry about yesterday.

CAROL. You should be.

ROGER. I overreacted.

CAROL. What?

ROGER. I overreacted.

CAROL. Hello?

ROGER. Shit.

CAROL. Where are you?

ROGER. In my car. Where are you?

CAROL. Lexington and 51st. I'm on my way to lunch.

ROGER. What? You're going in and out.

CAROL. Your phone sucks.

ROGER. It's not my phone. It's your phone.

CAROL. What?

ROGER. It's your phone that sucks. Look, can you meet me at Mom's tonight?! I have a compromise!

(Through ROGER's *phone, we hear the following.)*

WOMAN V.O. At the next corner, make a right.

CAROL. Who was that?

ROGER. It's my navigation system.

CAROL. Oh, I thought you picked up a hooker.

ROGER. Yeah, right. Look, can you meet me at seven?

CAROL. Make it eight.

ROGER. Eight's no good. I have a meeting in the city that ends at five-thirty. It's too much time to kill.

CAROL. So go buy a hat.

ROGER. I don't need a hat.

CAROL. Well, I have to go home after work and feed Lisa first.

ROGER. She's almost eighteen, she can't feed herself?

CAROL. You know what, just forget the whole thing.

ROGER. All right. All right. How's seven-thirty?

CAROL. What?

ROGER. Seven-thirty.

CAROL. Hey, fuck you, jerk-off.

ROGER. All right. Eight o'clock.

CAROL. Not you. A cab driver almost ran over my foot. I'll meet you at seven forty-five.

WOMAN V.O. At the second light, make a left…

Scene Three

(EVELYN's kitchen, that same evening. EVELYN crosses from the sink toward the hallway. She stops and glances at the piano bench. She sits down, plays a phrase and gets lost in thought. Lights dim, then come up downstage to reveal a young, very pregnant EVELYN and her husband, BENNY.)

BENNY. So, Evelyn, what do you think?

YOUNG EVELYN. Well…

BENNY. I think we should grab it.

YOUNG EVELYN. I don't know. It's a little out of our range. A hundred and ten dollars a month.

BENNY. Yeah, but look what we get. Three bedrooms, an elevator, schools nearby, walking distance to Sunset Park – you know how much I love that park. It even comes with friendly neighbors, Rose and Sal.

(in an Italian accent)

I'm Sal from Monteriggioni.

YOUNG EVELYN. They seemed like nice people, but I still think maybe we should start with a smaller place. Then if we have another baby, we can get something bigger.

BENNY. I'll be bringing in more money before you know it. My father's all the time talking about making me a partner in the butcher shop.

YOUNG EVELYN. Meantime, he's walking around the store like King Tut and you're plucking chickens.

BENNY. It's going to happen. You'll see. He just wants me to pay my dues. Learn the business inside out. Just like he did with his father.

YOUNG EVELYN. Well, maybe we should wait until then. It won't be such a stretch.

BENNY. Look, sometimes you've got to take a chance in life. This place is perfect, it's available immediately and it'll get us away from my parents, just like you want.

YOUNG EVELYN. Don't say it that way. It's not a question of getting away from them. I like your parents.

BENNY. You like my mother. But, let's face it, my father drives you crazy.

YOUNG EVELYN. He drives you crazy, too.

BENNY. I know.

YOUNG EVELYN. Then why are you saying it's me that wants to get away from him?

BENNY. That's just the way it came out. It's bad for both of us to be living with them.

YOUNG EVELYN. Well, we are all on top of each other in that little apartment. And once Eleanor comes, it's going to get even worse.

BENNY. Who's Eleanor?

YOUNG EVELYN. *(patting her stomach)* Eleanor. For Roosevelt.

BENNY. First of all, I still think it's a boy. And second, if we're going to name the baby after somebody famous, it should be somebody good-looking.

YOUNG EVELYN. That's ridiculous.

BENNY. It's a superstition from the old country.

YOUNG EVELYN. You're not from the old country.

BENNY. Growing up in my house, I might as well have been. I've got remnants. What happened to 'Carol'? Didn't we say if it was a girl, we'd name her Carol after your grandma?

YOUNG EVELYN. I still like that.

BENNY. Then it's settled. If it's a girl, Carol. If it's a boy, Errol. Errol Flynn Horowitz.

YOUNG EVELYN. You better be kidding. Ooh, the baby just moved. Here, feel.

(She takes his hand and puts it on her stomach.)

BENNY. Whoa. Got a regular little bucking bronco in there. Amazing how the time goes by. Feels like just yesterday I asked you to marry me.

YOUNG EVELYN. On the roller coaster at Coney Island.

BENNY. Hey, any schmuck can get down on one knee.

*(**EVELYN** laughs and kisses him.)*

YOUNG EVELYN. And now look at me.

(She pats her stomach.)

BENNY. The first of many, I hope.

YOUNG EVELYN. Not too many. I want a family not an army.

BENNY. I love this place.

(putting his arm around her)

Come on, what do you say?

YOUNG EVELYN. Well…

BENNY. I got the deposit right here. It's burning a hole in my pocket. And, baby, these are new pants…

YOUNG EVELYN. Okay. If you think we can swing it. And if it doesn't work out, we can always move.

BENNY. That's my little optimist.

(They kiss.)

ROGER *(O.S.)* Mom…

(Downstage lights dim. Lights up on **EVELYN** *still seated at the kitchen table as* **ROGER** *comes through the front door.)*

ROGER. Mom…

EVELYN. Hi.

(He kisses her.)

ROGER. How are you?

EVELYN. Since yesterday? About the same. Carol called, she's on her way.

ROGER. Good.

EVELYN. But when she gets here, I don't want the two of you starting in again. You're brother and sister, you only have each other. If we can't work this out in a calm and reasonable way, it's not worth doing. I don't care how much money anybody makes.

ROGER. It'll be fine, I promise.

EVELYN. You hungry?

ROGER. I could eat.

EVELYN. I'll make you something. After you called, I picked up some cold cuts.

ROGER. You didn't have to do that.

EVELYN. It was no trouble.

(**EVELYN** *crosses to the refrigerator and opens the door.*)

EVELYN. I've got turkey, corned beef, pastrami, roast beef, cole slaw, potato salad and the knishes you like.

ROGER. As long as you didn't go to any trouble. Let me have half turkey, half roast beef on...

EVELYN. I've got rye, egg and pumpernickel.

ROGER. Rye.

EVELYN. Swiss, cheddar or muenster?

ROGER. Cheddar.

EVELYN. Regular mustard, deli or dijon?

ROGER. Deli. And ask the busboy to bring some pickles.

(**EVELYN** *makes* **ROGER** *a sandwich.*)

ROGER. Look, Mom, I shouldn't have stormed out of here yesterday. I know it upset you.

EVELYN. I was up half the night.

ROGER. It's just that when Carol lays into me about how lucky I am that I married money, it drives me crazy. Believe me, there's plenty of downside to working for Allison's father. Last week, the old man comes into my office and says he's giving me a promotion; I'll be in charge of launching the company's newest hotel.

EVELYN. That's wonderful.

ROGER. Ask me where it is.

EVELYN. Where is it?

ROGER. Phnom Penh.

EVELYN. Cambodia? You're moving to Cambodia?

ROGER. No. I just have to go there a few times the first year, to get the place off the ground. The problem is, how the hell am I supposed to tap into the tourist business? 'Would you like a room with a view of The Killing Fields? Or something overlooking the Genocide Museum.'

EVELYN. Oy.

ROGER. That's the kind of thing her father does to me over and over again. Dangles a carrot on a stick, then shoves the carrot up my butt.

EVELYN. Maybe it's time you went off your own.

ROGER. Believe me, if I could, I would. But where am I going to make the kind of money I'm making there?

EVELYN. Maybe you don't need to make as much as you think you do.

ROGER. That's where you're wrong.

EVELYN. If you ask me, Allison pushes you too much.

ROGER. Let's not get into that again. All I'm saying is, my life is not as terrific as Carol makes it out to be. Because of her situation, she has no perspective.

EVELYN. Why don't you have some compassion for her?

ROGER. I do. I'm here, aren't I?

EVELYN. Eat.

(EVELYN *puts a thick sandwich down in front of* ROGER.)

ROGER. Aren't you going to eat?

EVELYN. I'll eat later. I'm waiting for Carol.

ROGER. Then why am I eating now?

EVELYN. You said you were hungry.

ROGER. Carol's not going to eat with us. She's eating with Lisa.

EVELYN. Why didn't you say something?

ROGER. I didn't know you were waiting for her. This sandwich is huge. Here, take half of it.

EVELYN. What you don't eat, you'll take home.

ROGER. Mom, just get a plate and take half the sandwich.

EVELYN. All right.

(As EVELYN *gets a plate,* ROGER *takes a bite of the sandwich.*)

ROGER. This is fantastic.

EVELYN. It's from Katz's.

ROGER. You went all the way into Manhattan to buy cold cuts?

EVELYN. It was no trouble.

(**EVELYN** *takes half the sandwich. The front door opens and* **CAROL** *enters using her key.*)

CAROL. *(handing* **EVELYN** *a twenty dollar bill)* Here's your twenty back.

EVELYN. What twenty?

CAROL. The one you stuck in my purse when I wasn't looking. You're eating without me?

EVELYN. Roger said you were eating with Lisa.

CAROL. I said I was feeding her, not eating with her.

(to **ROGER***)*

I knew she'd have food.

ROGER. She went to Katz's.

CAROL. You went all the way to Manhattan to buy deli?

EVELYN. It was no trouble.

(to **CAROL***)*

What can I make you? I have turkey, pastrami...

CAROL. I'll make my own. You eat. Ma, you want some water?

EVELYN. No.

ROGER. I could use a little water.

CAROL. Sure.

(**CAROL** *pours herself a glass of filtered water and pours* **ROGER** *a glass of cloudy tap water. He reacts when she gives him his water, but decides to move on.*)

ROGER. So, Carol, how's Lisa doing?

CAROL. Lisa, Roger, is doing fine.

ROGER. School going okay for her?

CAROL. It's great. She's getting straight A's. She's probably going to be valedictorian.

ROGER. That's terrific. My kids are challenging the world record for academic probation. And that's after we spent a small fortune on tutors. For a while there, I thought we'd have to sell the house to pay for them.

CAROL. *(crossing to the table with plate and a jar of mustard)* As long as you didn't have to sell your navigation system…

(ROGER glares at CAROL. EVELYN jumps in an attempt to diffuse an argument.)

EVELYN. Well, here we are. The three of us having dinner together. I can't remember the last time that happened.

(ROGER and CAROL eat in silence.)

EVELYN. It's just like the old days, when you were children.

CAROL. Yeah, the only thing missing is some strange kid playing 'The Happy Farmer' on the piano in the background.

EVELYN. They weren't strange kids. They were my piano students.

CAROL. Ma, they were strange.

(CAROL dips a rolled up piece of turkey into the jar of mustard.)

EVELYN. Put the mustard on a plate. Eat like a person.

CAROL. I'm sorry. I forgot that you like dinner to be formal.

(CAROL puts some mustard on a plate.)

CAROL. Roger, remember that big fat kid, the one stuffed into the Boy Scout uniform; the time he sat down and collapsed the piano bench? What was his name?

ROGER. Steven.

EVELYN. Steven Snyder. His mother was a shoe model at Lord and Taylor.

CAROL. And what about that strange girl with all the allergies? Her nose was always dripping mucous. And what was that rash she had all over her body?

EVELYN. She had eczema, the poor thing. I can't remember her name...

ROGER. Very appetizing, eating while she was here.

CAROL. After she left I had to wipe her ointments off the keys before I could sit down and play.

EVELYN. Meanwhile, those lessons brought in money we needed after your father died.

CAROL. I'm thinking they would have brought in the same money if you'd left the piano in the living room.

EVELYN. Albeit unconventional, moving the piano in here made a lot of sense. I could give lessons, make dinner and keep an eye on the two of you at the same time.

CAROL. And the piano is still here because...?

EVELYN. Because it's my house and I like it here. Who wants coffee? I'll make a fresh pot.

ROGER. As long as it's decaf.

CAROL. Same here.

EVELYN. This time of night, I'd serve you regular? Barbara.

(CAROL *and* ROGER *exchange a concerned look.*)

CAROL. (*correcting her*) Carol.

EVELYN. I know your name. Barbara was the student with eczema.

(EVELYN *gets up and makes a pot of coffee.*)

ROGER. (*to* CAROL) So, let me tell you my idea.

CAROL. I'm all ears.

ROGER. If we buy the apartment, when we eventually sell it, I'm okay with splitting the profits, fifty-fifty.

CAROL. Really?

ROGER. Yeah. Allison and I talked about it, and we both think that's fair.

CAROL. Great.

ROGER. But...

CAROL. Yes?

ROGER. If the loan's going to be in my name, and the responsibility is all on my shoulders, this is what I'm proposing. I'll put down ten percent, and you'll reimburse me for fifty percent of it when we sell. I'll take out a loan for the balance, which is, two hundred and twenty-five thousand dollars, and we'll split the monthly interest payments equally.

CAROL. I see your lips moving, but I have no idea what you're saying. Just cut to the chase. How much is this going to cost me?

*(**ROGER** takes a sheet of paper out of his briefcase.)*

ROGER. With a thirty year fixed, the payments are twelve-seventeen-thirty-four. So, your share of the monthly payment would come out to six-o-eight-sixty-seven.

CAROL. Are you kidding? I can't afford an extra six hundred dollars a month.

EVELYN. So you'll take my rent money.

CAROL. No.

ROGER. *(to **CAROL**)* What can you afford? Comfortably?

CAROL. Comfortably? Nothing.

ROGER. Which puts us right back where we started.

CAROL. All right, look, I understand you shouldn't be the one to take on everything. But I'm stuck here. I make what I make. Even if I put in overtime, I can't come up with an extra six hundred dollars a month.

EVELYN. Unless…

CAROL. Give it up, Ma. I am not taking your money.

EVELYN. Unless…I do something I promised Aunt Sophie I wouldn't do.

CAROL. How did Aunt Sophie get in the middle of this?

EVELYN. Because when she died, she left you a little inheritance.

CAROL. Yeah, right. You're making that up.

*(**EVELYN** crosses to a drawer and fishes out a bank book. She hands it to **CAROL** who opens it.)*

CAROL. *(reading)* In trust for...Holy shit. She left me ten thousand dollars.

ROGER. How much did she leave me?

EVELYN. Nothing. You, she wasn't worried about.

ROGER. What the fuck?

CAROL. I have ten thousand dollars!

EVELYN. *(to* **ROGER***)* You could look at it as a compliment.

ROGER. I don't.

EVELYN. I'm sorry. What can I say? She wasn't herself at the end.

CAROL. Aunt Sophie died three years ago. Why didn't you give me this then?

EVELYN. Because there was a stipulation. I was to put the money away and not tell you about it until you re-married.

CAROL. That's a ridiculous stipulation. I need the money when I'm not married, not when I'm re-married. And who the hell was she to come up with a stipulation like that anyway? She was an old maid. How could you honor that?

EVELYN. She was my only sister. It was her dying wish. I tried to talk her out of it, but it's hard to reason with somebody who's drifting in and out of consciousness.

ROGER. I can't believe she didn't leave me anything.

EVELYN. She felt the money should go to Carol because she needed it the most.

CAROL. Why was it such a secret? If it was supposed to be an incentive for me to remarry, why wouldn't you tell me?

EVELYN. She made me swear not to. She wanted to be sure you married for love, not money.

CAROL. This is insane.

EVELYN. I know my sister was a little crazy, and I did what she wanted for as long as I could. But you need the money now, so that's it. I'm over-ruling her dying wish.

ROGER. Aunt Sophie never liked me. I always had that feeling.

EVELYN. What are you saying? She loved you.

ROGER. I think she had a problem with men. I think she was gay.

EVELYN. My sister was not gay…Or, maybe she was. She did own a lot of slacks. Who knows? Back then, you didn't announce it.

CAROL. I can't believe it. Out of nowhere, I have ten thousand dollars. I can pay off my credit card bill, maybe get my eyes done…

ROGER. Whoa. Whoa. Whoa. Remember what we were just talking about? Buying the apartment.

CAROL. I know.

ROGER. Then why are we talking about plastic surgery?

CAROL. Because I'm a middle-aged divorced woman with drooping eyelids.

ROGER. Be that as it may, you've only got ten thousand dollars. If you do your eyes and pay off your bills, how much do you think you'll have left?

EVELYN. Roger's right. You should think about your priorities.

CAROL. Okay. Forget my eyes. I'll put part of the money toward bills and use the rest to pay my share of the monthly payments on the loan.

EVELYN. That sounds reasonable.

ROGER. Yes and no.

(*to* **CAROL**)

Under the circumstances, it's also fair that you be responsible for part of the down payment.

CAROL. That wasn't the deal.

ROGER. The deal was proposed before you became the sole heir of Aunt Sophie's estate. The down payment is ten percent of the overall price, so you should put up a thousand dollars.

EVELYN. Now you're getting carried away. Don't take it out on Carol because you're mad at Aunt Sophie.

ROGER. I'm not.

(The telephone rings. **EVELYN** *crosses to the phone and picks up the cordless handset)*

EVELYN. *(into phone)* Hello…Yes, it is….Tomorrow? Which school?

CAROL. *(to* **ROGER***)* Look, if the thousand dollars is so important to you, you can have it. I don't want to keep fighting about this.

ROGER. Neither do I. It's just the principle of the thing.

EVELYN. Where is that, Bay Ridge?…What grade?

ROGER. I'll tell you what, how about we compromise? Give me five hundred.

CAROL. Fine.

EVELYN. Say it again. What are the cross-streets?

CAROL. I won't be able to make a dent in my credit card but I'll have enough to make loan payments for a year, maybe two…

EVELYN. Hold on a second. I've got people over. Let me go where I can hear you.

*(***EVELYN*** crosses into another room.)*

CAROL. Meanwhile, I can work overtime and start saving up. Or work at my friend's booth at the flea market.

ROGER. Okay. Okay. Pack up your violin. Forget the five hundred. Make it two-fifty.

CAROL. Thank you.

ROGER. You're welcome. Could you get the coffee?

*(***CAROL*** crosses to the coffee pot and pours a cup for ***ROGER*** and herself.)*

ROGER. So here's what we do. First thing tomorrow morning we turn in the letter of intent to buy. Then I go to the bank and start the paper work on a loan.

CAROL. You're absolutely positive that this is a good investment?

ROGER. Yes. How many times do I have to tell you?

CAROL. I need reassuring. Taking this on is a huge financial step for me.

ROGER. I guarantee you, Carol, in fifteen years this apartment will have doubled in value.

CAROL. Fifteen years? Are you serious? I'll be making loan
payments for fifteen years?

ROGER. I'm just picking a number. We may not have to hold
onto it for that long. I mean, what are the chances of
Mom being in this place for another fifteen years?

CAROL. Knowing her, she could be here for a hundred.

(CAROL *crosses to the refrigerator and opens it.*)

CAROL. There's no milk.

ROGER. I can't drink black.

CAROL. You're such a baby.

(*Unseen by* CAROL *and* ROGER, EVELYN *starts to enter
during the next speech. She overhears the conversation
and steps back out of view.*)

ROGER. Look, let's be realistic. She's seventy-five years old.
You factor in the heart condition that she may or may
not have, who knows what we're facing.

CAROL. This is such a weird thing to be talking about. Basically, what we're saying is, the sooner she goes, the
sooner we cash out.

ROGER. Technically, yes. But we can't look at it like that.
And there are other things that could happen.

CAROL. Such as?

ROGER. People her age have strokes, fall down, break
things. Truth is, she may not be able to stay in this
apartment for the rest of her life.

CAROL. There's a conversation I'm looking forward to
having with her.

ROGER. I know it wouldn't be easy. But at some point you
have to do what you have to do. And if the best place
for her is a nursing home, that may be a decision we
have to make. Out near me, there are some incredible
places. One of them looks like a country club.

CAROL. If that's the road we're going down, let's hope she's
in a coma. Because to get Mom there, we're going to
have to tie her up and stick her on your roof rack.

ROGER. It's probably how nine out of ten people arrive.

(EVELYN *enters.*)

EVELYN. The deal's off. We're not buying.

ROGER. What?

EVELYN. We're not buying. So you don't have to worry about when I die, or putting me into a Goddamn home.

CAROL. Ma…

EVELYN. How dare the two of you sit in my kitchen and talk about such things?

CAROL. You don't understand.

EVELYN. I heard every word you said.

ROGER. It wasn't a real discussion. It was hypothetical.

EVELYN. Call it whatever you want. Meanwhile, you'll buy the place and the next thing I know, you're selling and I'm being confined against my will.

ROGER. First of all, we're just putting up the money. The apartment still has to be in your name.

EVELYN. I'm sure that's a great disappointment to you.

ROGER. Mom, we can't make you do anything you don't want to do.

EVELYN. Unless you have me declared incompetent.

CAROL. You're getting a little crazy.

EVELYN. See, there it is. It's starting already.

ROGER. Mom…

EVELYN. Mom? Who's Mom? I'm not Mom anymore. Now I'm a commodity.

CAROL. You're not a commodity.

EVELYN. Oh, no? You're waiting for me die so you can cash out.

CAROL. I didn't mean it the way you're taking it.

ROGER. She was kidding around.

EVELYN. In other words, my life is a big joke to you.

CAROL. Will you take it easy?

EVELYN. I hope that, when the two of you are my age, your kids treat you the same way. You'll see what it feels like.

CAROL. Ma, please, sit down and let's talk about this.

EVELYN. You're not controlling my future. Nobody is.

    (**EVELYN** *grabs her coat and starts to put it on.*)

CAROL. Where are you going?

EVELYN. For milk.

CAROL. Now?

EVELYN. Now is when I need it.

ROGER. I'll go.

EVELYN. I don't need you to do it for me.

ROGER. Then I'll go with you. You shouldn't go at night by yourself.

EVELYN. It's seven-thirty, Goddamn it. I don't need a body-guard. And I'll tell you another thing, I will never, ever let either of you have power over me. To my death bed, I'll fight it. In fact, I'm going to make it easy for you – I'm moving to Italy.

CAROL. Italy?

EVELYN. Monteriggioni. That's where Sal is buried. Rose has always wanted to go back there and she asked me to go with her. The family still has property there.

ROGER. You're a Jew from Brooklyn. What are you going to do in Italy?

EVELYN. It's beautiful there and they respect the old.

CAROL. Ma, you're not making any sense.

EVELYN. To you. I'm going out and I don't want either one of you here when I get back.

    (**EVELYN** *exits, slamming the door behind her.*)

EVELYN. (*O.S.*) (*yelling*) Over my dead body, you'll put me in a nursing home.

    (**CAROL** *and* **ROGER** *look at each other.*)

CAROL. What just happened?

ROGER. I have no idea.

CAROL. It's like from out of nowhere she lost her mind.

ROGER. It's your fault.

CAROL. My fault?

ROGER. 'The sooner she goes, the sooner we cash out'?
You had her tied to my roof rack.

CAROL. I thought we were having a private conversation.

ROGER. She was right in the other room.

CAROL. Excuse me, but you didn't have any problem throwing in your two cents. You already had her in a nursing
home.

*(There's a knock at the door. They both cross to open it.
It's* ROSE.*)*

ROSE. Is everything all right? I heard the door slam.

CAROL. We had a little disagreement with Mom and she
stormed out.

ROSE. Sounded like more than a little disagreement. What
was she yelling about a nursing home?

ROGER. We were talking about buying the apartment...and
what could happen in the natural course of things –

CAROL. She overheard us say the words 'nursing home'
and went crazy.

ROSE. You were talking about putting her into a nursing
home?

CAROL. No. I mean, not now. You know, should something
happen in the future. She took the whole thing out of
context.

*(*ROSE *shakes her head.)*

ROGER. Rose, what's this about you and my mother going
to Italy? She said that you're planning on moving to
the town where Sal is from.

ROSE. We've talked about it. The last time was maybe six
months ago. But we never made a definite plan. She
said we were going?

CAROL. Yes.

ROSE. Well, I don't know how that's possible.

CAROL. She said you had property there.

ROSE. Sal's family does. But I couldn't go now if I wanted
to. Connie wants me to come live with her.

CAROL. What?

ROSE. I'm going to go live with Connie.

ROGER. Connie?

ROSE. In Los Angeles.

CAROL. You're moving?

ROSE. I am.

ROGER. Wow.

CAROL. Holy shit. You're leaving the building?

(**ROSE** *nods.*)

ROGER. When?

ROSE. At the end of the month.

CAROL. Oh, my God, Rose. You and Mom are…fixtures. It won't be the same…not having you across the hall.

ROSE. I know, sweetheart.

ROGER. Wait a minute. I don't get it. If you're going to Los Angeles, why does she think the two of you are going to Italy? Maybe she really is starting to lose it.

ROSE. She's not losing anything. I haven't told her yet.

ROGER. When were you planning on telling her?

ROSE. I was waiting for the right time.

ROGER. And when would that be? When the moving van pulls up?

ROSE. Of course not.

CAROL. Roger, lighten up. This can't be an easy thing for her.

ROSE. It's not. We've been together for over fifty years. I'm the one she confides in. And now she's going to be here by herself.

CAROL. Well, Rose, she's not exactly by herself. She still has us.

ROSE. You visit, but with all due respect…

CAROL. What?

ROSE. Look what happens when you try to talk to her.

CAROL. We had a fight. We've had lots of fights.

ROSE. Meanwhile, she's wandering the streets alone at night.

CAROL. She overreacted.

ROSE. And why do you think that was?

CAROL. Because…I don't know. That's what we're trying to figure out.

ROSE. You don't know because she doesn't tell you everything.

ROGER. Rose, what's going on with her? Do you know something that we don't know?

ROSE. It's not my place to say. All I can tell you is, your mother carries a lot inside.

(ROSE turns and starts for the door.)

CAROL. Rose, what does that mean?

ROSE. I'm sorry. Talk to her.

(She exits.)

ACT TWO

Scene One

(The stage is dark.)

DR. GOLDSTEIN. *(answering his cell phone)* Hello?

CAROL. Dr. Goldstein. This is Carol, Evelyn Horowitz's daughter. I'm really sorry to bother you...

(From his end of the call, casino sounds can be heard in the background.)

DR. GOLDSTEIN. It's all right. What's wrong?

CAROL. I know you saw my mother not long ago, I just want to know – is she okay?

DR. GOLDSTEIN. Well, she's got a little arthritis in her hands and she needs to watch her blood pressure, but other than that...Is she having a problem?

CAROL. Nothing specific. She just seems off, agitated...

DR. GOLDSTEIN. She was fine when I saw her. As a matter of fact, as she was leaving, I told her, 'I wish I had your energy.'

CAROL. So, there's nothing major going on.

DR. GOLDSTEIN. No. But if you're worried, have her call for an appointment. I'll be back from my symposium on Wednesday.

(We hear the sound of somebody hitting the jackpot on a slot machine.)

DR. GOLDSTEIN. I'm between lectures.

CAROL. Right. Thanks. And good luck.

Scene Two

(CAROL paces then opens the refrigerator. She stares inside but takes nothing. ROGER enters.)

ROGER. She back?

CAROL. No.

ROGER. I couldn't find her.

CAROL. Where'd you look?

ROGER. Everywhere, starting with Shapiro's. Did you know a Pakastani guy owns that place now? I described her and he said she'd been in there about an hour ago and bought a container of milk. I walked around the whole neighborhood and there's no sign of her. And she's not answering her cell phone.

CAROL. Her cell phone?

ROGER. Yeah, the one I bought her last year.

(CAROL crosses to the piano bench and takes out EVE-LYN's cell phone.)

CAROL. It's never left the piano bench.

ROGER. Did you reach the doctor?

CAROL. Yeah. He said there's nothing wrong with her.

ROGER. Well, that's good.

CAROL. I'm going to call the police.

ROGER. And tell them what? Your seventy-five year-old mother ran away from home?

CAROL. Well, we can't just sit here and do nothing.

ROGER. All right. Let's both go look for her. You walk towards Fourth, I'll walk towards Fort Hamilton.

CAROL. Why don't we just take your car?

ROGER. We're much better off on foot. We can look in doorways, alleys…

CAROL. You got a spot right in front of the building, didn't you?

ROGER. That has nothing to do with it.

(EVELYN's phone rings and ROGER quickly grabs it.)

ROGER. Hello. Hi, Lisa.

(ROGER *hands the phone to* CAROL.)

CAROL. *(into the phone)* ...No, Grandma's not here...to the store...Lisa, it's not a good time...Oh, shit. I forgot to ask her...I'll get it. I'll bring it home...I won't forget. All right, bye.

(She hangs up.)

ROGER. Bring what home?

CAROL. That old coat with the fur collar Ma used to wear. She's in the school play –

(EVELYN *enters. She carries a container of milk.*)

EVELYN. What are you still doing here?

CAROL. We were worried about you. Where have you been?

EVELYN. I got my milk, I went to the park...

ROGER. Alone? At night?

EVELYN. I told you, I can take care of myself.

CAROL. It's freezing out there.

EVELYN. It wasn't that bad.

CAROL. Ma, you're shivering.

(ROGER *gets an afghan to put around her.*)

ROGER. Come over here and sit down.

CAROL. I'll make you some tea.

(CAROL *puts a cup of hot water in a counter-top microwave.*)

ROGER. How can you go to the park by yourself at night? You could have been attacked, raped.

EVELYN. Nice talk, your mother being raped.

ROGER. I'm just saying, it's dangerous.

EVELYN. I had to go someplace I could think. I needed to calm myself down and look at the whole situation logically. I was very upset when I said I don't want to buy the apartment and I'm moving to Italy with Rose. But upon reflection, I know exactly what it is I'm going to do. I don't want to buy the apartment and I'm moving to Italy with Rose.

CAROL. Mom –

EVELYN. I sat on the same bench that your father and I used to sit on. So many times we used to talk about going with Rose and Sal to Sal's hometown. Your father and Sal, from the second they met, they were like brothers. Sal was hoping, maybe one day, he and Rose would retire there. And your father said if the place was as wonderful as Sal made it sound, maybe we'd retire there, too. Well, the men are gone now, and for me and Rose, maybe this will be a way to keep that dream alive.

(CAROL and ROGER exchange a worried look. EVELYN notices.)

EVELYN. I know it's going to a big change for everybody, but it doesn't mean we won't see each other. Nowadays, people go back and forth to Europe like it's around the corner. You'll bring the kids. It'll be very educational.

(CAROL hands EVELYN her tea, then she and ROGER sit on either side of EVELYN.)

CAROL. Ma, Rose can't go to Italy. She's going to live with Connie.

EVELYN. What are you talking about?

CAROL. Rose said Connie wants her to move to Los Angeles.

EVELYN. When did she tell you that?

ROGER. She heard you yelling when you left and she came over. We told her what you said about Italy and that's when she told us she was moving.

EVELYN. *(dismissive)* She won't go.

CAROL. Ma, she's going. She's moving to Los Angeles.

EVELYN. It doesn't make any sense. I was with her yesterday, she never mentioned a thing.

CAROL. She said that she didn't know how to tell you.

EVELYN. Whenever she comes back from there, all she does is complain about the smog, and the earthquakes and the cockamamie pizza with the pineapple on top. If you don't drive there, you're trapped.

CAROL. I guess she's willing to deal with all that for what she'll get in return.

EVELYN. I don't believe it.

ROGER. We didn't believe it either, but it's true. She's really going.

(**EVELYN** *is stopped cold as it finally sinks in.*)

EVELYN. Some friend she turned out to be. You think after fifty years you'd know somebody.

CAROL. Look, this is a shock for all of us. But from Rose's point of view, it does make sense. She's almost eighty, she's got one daughter and she wants to be with her.

(**EVELYN** *shakes her head in disgust.*)

CAROL. I know how hard this is for you. You and Rose have been so close. You've always relied on each other.

EVELYN. I don't rely on anybody. If she wants to move to Los Angeles, goodbye and good luck. I'll be fine. It's like I always say, you're born alone, you die alone.

ROGER. You're not alone. Carol and I are here.

EVELYN. And I know what your plans for me are. Lock me up and throw away the key.

ROGER. We're not going to put you in a nursing home.

EVELYN. Until you need money.

CAROL. We would never do that to you.

EVELYN. That's not what you said before.

CAROL. Ma, even if you get sick, we'll find a way to keep you here. I promise.

EVELYN. I don't believe you.

ROGER. What do you want us to do, put it in writing? We'll never put you in a nursing home. I swear.

EVELYN. I don't trust you.

ROGER. I swear on my kids.

EVELYN. I still don't trust you.

(**CAROL,** *angrily, rises.*)

CAROL. Jesus Christ. What's it going to take? Why would we lie to you? What the hell is wrong with you?

ROGER. Take it easy.

CAROL. No. How offensive is this? I'm not going to stand here and be insulted.

(*to* **EVELYN**)

We're your children. Our word means nothing to you? It makes me sick.

(**EVELYN** *drops her head and starts to cry.*)

ROGER. Ma, don't.

(*to* **CAROL**)

Now look what you did.

(**ROGER** *puts his arm around* **EVELYN.**)

ROGER. Ma, it'll be okay.

EVELYN. I killed him…

ROGER. What?

EVELYN. Your father. I killed your father.

(**ROGER** *and* **CAROL** *are stunned.* **CAROL** *crosses back to the table. Lights dim then come up downstage to reveal, a tired and subdued* **EVELYN,** *age thirty-two. She peels potatoes at a small kitchen table.* **BENNY** *enters, hiding something behind his back. He leans in and kisses* **YOUNG EVELYN.**)

BENNY. Hiya, baby doll.

YOUNG EVELYN. Hi.

BENNY. Where are the kids?

YOUNG EVELYN. Across the hall. Sal got Rose a colored television, with one of those big screens, fifteen inches.

BENNY. Well, I got you something.

(**BENNY** *presents* **EVELYN** *with a bunch of flowers.*)

YOUNG EVELYN. They're beautiful. I wish I had the strength to put them in a vase.

BENNY. Tough day?

YOUNG EVELYN. You could say that.

BENNY. The kids?

YOUNG EVELYN. Your father.

BENNY. What happened?

YOUNG EVELYN. Well, it seems that when we moved him in here, I forgot to send a change of address to the Knights of Pythias. Now his dues are in arrears seven months, and he has to pay a fourteen dollar penalty.

BENNY. So, we'll cover it.

YOUNG EVELYN. I told him that. But he said I had no idea the damage I had done to his reputation…Then he called me useless.

BENNY. I'm really sorry. I hate that he keeps lashing out at you like that. I'll talk to him again. God, I had no idea it was going to be this hard having him here.

YOUNG EVELYN. I know.

BENNY. My father is used to being waited on hand and foot. That's what my mother did rather than fight with him.

(**ABE** *enters. He's an old seventy with emphysema and he walks with a cane. During this scene, he occasionally struggles for breath.*)

ABE. What are you doing home so early?

BENNY. I left Harry to close up.

ABE. Stupid. Giving him a responsibility like that.

BENNY. Dad, he's been working at the store forever. He knows how to close the door and shut off the lights.

ABE. Stupid.

(**ABE** *notices potatoes on table.*)

ABE. Potatoes again?

(*mumbling in Yiddish*)

A finsternish.

YOUNG EVELYN. What?

ABE. I said, we're having potatoes again?

YOUNG EVELYN. Abe, when you moved in you said, I'm a simple man. I like my meat and I like my potatoes.

ABE. Meat you have everyday. Potatoes you need a break from. It's Friday night. We should be having kugel.

BENNY. She's already peeling potatoes, Dad. We're having potatoes.

YOUNG EVELYN. I'll make a kugel next week.

ABE. *(to* **BENNY***)* How was business today?

BENNY. Good.

ABE. What'd you take in?

BENNY. Enough.

ABE. You're lying. I can see it on your face.

BENNY. It was a little slow.

ABE. Friday's used to be the best days. Goddamn A & P. Killing business all over the city.

   (to **YOUNG EVELYN***)*

   Didn't your parents have a candy store?

YOUNG EVELYN. Yes, Abe.

ABE. The big chains would have wiped them right out. They're lucky they're dead.

YOUNG EVELYN. You know what they say, there's always a silver lining.

ABE. I should come back to work.

BENNY. You can hardly make it across the room.

ABE. I'm sick of the two of you treating me like I'm some kind of invalid. I'm a little short of breath once in a while, that's all. What's the big deal? I don't even know what I'm doing here. I should be back in my own place, above the store. Then I could still come down, see the customers, spread some goodwill.

YOUNG EVELYN. You're here because you couldn't make it up the one flight of stairs.

BENNY. And if we didn't watch you from morning till night, you'd still be smoking ten cigars a day.

YOUNG EVELYN. Speaking of which, Rose says she smelled smoke coming from the stairway today.

ABE. Maybe there was a fire.

YOUNG EVELYN. It was cigar smoke.

ABE. It wasn't me.

BENNY. Are you trying to kill yourself? You're still smoking with emphysema?

ABE. I wasn't smoking. You're going to take the word of that fishwife over mine?

YOUNG EVELYN. Rose is my friend and I resent you calling her that.

ABE. She should mind her own Goddamn business. Women today. You know who I blame? The husbands. A generation of spineless nebishes.

(to **BENNY***)*

Take you. You're a butcher. Did you ever slaughter a cow?

BENNY. What?

ABE. You were brought up in a kosher home, your wife's not religious, so it's Friday night and there's no Shabbos.

YOUNG EVELYN. Abe, I told you, if it's important to you, I will light the candles.

ABE. It's not necessary. I'll adjust to that, just like I adjust to everything else. I came here as a boy from Russia, didn't speak the language, didn't have a pot to piss in, I adjusted. My wife of forty five years dies, I'm adjusting. My only child and his wife, Mrs. Trotsky, want to keep me a prisoner in their home, I'll adjust to that too.

*(***ABE*** turns and crosses off.* **BENNY** *puts his arm around* **YOUNG EVELYN***.)*

BENNY. I'm going to go talk to him. It'll get better. I promise.

(Lights dim downstage and come up on **EVELYN**, **CAROL** *and* **ROGER** *seated at the kitchen table.)*

EVELYN. It didn't get better. It only got worse. Another supermarket opened nearby and your father had to work night and day to keep the customers he had left. Some nights he'd come home, he didn't even have the strength to eat. He'd go right to bed. Meanwhile, Grandpa was getting sicker and sicker. There was so much tension in the house, I thought I'd lose my mind.

CAROL. I remember how Grandpa used to treat you.

EVELYN. You do? You were only nine. A little girl.

CAROL. It was pretty extreme. He was always barking at you, ordering you around like you were his maid.

ROGER. I remember the fights you and Dad used to have about him. Especially that big one on the fire escape.

EVELYN. We didn't want to fight in front of you.

CAROL. That one was awful.

EVELYN. You heard everything?

CAROL. We couldn't make out the words, but you and Dad never yelled at each other like that before. We went to sleep that night convinced you were going to get divorced.

ROGER. You went to sleep. I was up. In the middle of the night, I had to go to the bathroom and I saw Dad sitting on the fire escape by himself. I knew it always cheered him up to talk about baseball, so I asked him how the Yankees did. He said they won. And then he told me how bad he felt that he'd been so busy, he couldn't take me to a game that year. He promised that the next summer he'd take me to a doubleheader.

EVELYN. But he never got to do it.

ROGER. No.

(Lights dim and come up downstage on **YOUNG EVELYN** *and* **BENNY**.*)*

YOUNG EVELYN. So we're agreed?

BENNY. We're agreed because you're insisting.

YOUNG EVELYN. I'm insisting because I'm the one that's trapped here taking care of him from the second I wake up in the morning to the second I go to bed. He can't bathe himself, he needs help going to the bathroom, you have to force him to take his medicine. It's too much.

BENNY. I know. I know what you do for him. You have most of the responsibility. Believe me, if there was more I could do, I would. But it's not exactly like I'm going to a picnic everyday.

YOUNG EVELYN. I understand that. We're both doing everything we can, but it's not enough. You yourself said he's getting to a point where he needs more care than we can give him.

BENNY. Maybe we can bring in some live-in help. A nurse or somebody.

YOUNG EVELYN. And put them where? You think your father's going to let somebody sleep in the room with him? We've been through this over and over again. There's no choice. Benny, please. We can't do it anymore.

(**ABE** *enters. He's in worse shape than when we last saw him.*)

ABE. *(to* **EVELYN***)* I need more cough drops. And don't get me the Smith Brothers, like last time. I want the Pine Brothers. The soft. And not the cherry. I want the honey.

BENNY. Dad, sit down a minute. We've got to talk.

ABE. About what?

BENNY. Just sit down, would you please?

ABE. Don't forget the cough drops.

(*They all sit.*)

ABE. What is it?

BENNY. Well…

ABE. So?

BENNY. Dad. You know how much we love you…

ABE. Do me a favor, you got something to say, just say it.

BENNY. After Mom died, we really thought the best thing would be for you to come live with us. But now…

ABE. Thank God. I'm going home.

(**BENNY** *shakes his head.*)

BENNY. No, Dad. You can't live by yourself. Your emphysema is getting worse. You're in constant pain from arthritis. It's hard for you to do the things you need to do to take care of yourself…With the two kids and everything else that's going on in our lives…it's just too much for us to handle.

(**BENNY** *takes a long pause.*)

YOUNG EVELYN. So Benny and I visited a place the other day.

BENNY. It's only ten minutes from here.

ABE. What kind of place?

BENNY. A beautiful place. Gorgeous grounds. Brand new building, with a big dining room.

ABE. You want to put me in a nursing home?

BENNY. It's not what you're thinking.

ABE. Then what is it?

BENNY. It's –

ABE. It's either a nursing home or it's not a nursing home.

BENNY. It's a home for the elderly.

ABE. That's the same thing.

BENNY. No it's not. Not everybody who goes there is sick.

ABE. Then why do they go?

BENNY. A lot of older people choose to move there because it's easier for them.

ABE. But you want me to move there because it's easier for you.

BENNY. Dad, I'm telling you, this place is unbelievable. They have all kinds of activities. They've got a Kosher kitchen, services on Fridays and Saturdays. And let's face it, you are sick. You can get physical therapy and –

ABE. *(to* **YOUNG EVELYN***)* This is all your doing. You put him up to it.

BENNY. She didn't put me up to anything. It's a mutual decision.

ABE. My ass. You think I don't know you're protecting her.

(to **YOUNG EVELYN***)*

If I was your father, you'd throw me out on the street like this?

YOUNG EVELYN. Abe, we're not throwing you out on the street. This is one of the best places in Brooklyn.

BENNY. You'll be nearby.

ABE. I'm nearby now.

BENNY. We'll come visit all the time, we'll bring the kids.

ABE. For what? To show them how you treat a parent like garbage? For a son to do this to a father – When I was growing up, a relative needed help, somebody had a problem, the door was always open. Somebody got sick, we took them in. At one point, we had nine people living in a two room apartment. Nobody complained, they did what they had to. We treated everybody with dignity. Why? Because the family was sacred.

(ABE is short of breath.)

BENNY. Dad, take it easy.

YOUNG EVELYN. Let me get you a glass of water.

(YOUNG EVELYN gets him a glass of water. She holds it out to him.)

ABE. From you, I want nothing.

(YOUNG EVELYN hands the glass to BENNY. BENNY hands it to ABE. He takes a drink and puts the glass down. He looks at BENNY.)

ABE. Take me to the river.

BENNY. Dad, stop it.

ABE. I said, take me to the river.

BENNY. You're not jumping in the river.

ABE. I wouldn't give you that satisfaction. I'm taking all of my money and I'm throwing it where you can't get your hands on it. Not one nickel from my savings is going toward you burying me alive.

BENNY. That's not what we're doing. And we're not going to touch your money. We'll pay for it. This is a great place. Just give it a chance.

(ABE is silent.)

YOUNG EVELYN. I'm sorry, Abe. If there was any other way…

ABE. The other way would have been if my son had married somebody with compassion, not a cold-hearted witch.

(ABE smashes his cane on the table. Lights dim and then come up, upstage.)

CAROL. Oh, my God. How could he say that to you?

EVELYN. Of all the terrible things he said to me, that was the worst. The next morning, I was ready for more of the same. But when we went to his room, we found him sitting on his bed. He was wearing his best suit, and even with those gnarled fingers he had somehow managed to tie his tie and put on cuff links. Then he looked at us with such hatred in his eyes and said, 'I'm ready to go.'

ROGER. And that was it?

EVELYN. Yes. He refused to spend another night under the same roof with us. All the way to the home, your father was sick to his stomach. And Grandpa made him feel even worse. He wouldn't look at him or talk to him. It was like that the whole time – while we were moving him in, putting his things away. And, then, when your father went to kiss him goodbye, Grandpa turned away and spit.

ROGER. That's horrible.

CAROL. Daddy must have been so hurt.

EVELYN. He was devastated. And riddled with guilt. It was so bad, he said he could never face the customers if they knew what he had done. So when they came into the store, he told them he had moved his father to Florida, that it was better for his health there. He insisted we tell that to everybody. The only ones outside the family who knew the truth were Rose and Sal.

CAROL. And Grandpa never adjusted to the home at all?

EVELYN. Not for one second. The people there took wonderful care of him. They tried to get him involved in activities, but he wouldn't give an inch. He isolated himself so much, they couldn't even get him to go to services.

ROGER. I think I remember going to visit him.

EVELYN. We took you both, once. We thought maybe seeing you, he'd perk up a little. But that day, he wouldn't even get out of bed. Why expose you to that? You were just children. After he had been there three months, the phone rang in the middle of the night. Your father answered it and turned white. I knew right away what had happened. Grandpa had died in his sleep. Your father cried for hours. Then never again. I was heartsick and felt like it was all my fault, that I should have been stronger and found a way to put up with Grandpa. Your father said he didn't blame me. But, I don't know…our relationship was never the same…There was this distance. We had always been so close…Then, six months to the day that Grandpa died, we were coming back from visiting the cemetery, and we were walking down Forty-Third Street. We were in front of Ebinger's. I said to him, why don't we go in and get that coffee cake you like, with the raisins. Before he could answer, right there on the street, he suddenly collapsed. I thought maybe he had fainted, but when I bent down, I knew right away. He was gone. At forty-two years old.

CAROL. It wasn't your fault, Ma.

ROGER. Dad had a heart attack.

EVELYN. Because of what happened.

ROGER. You don't know that.

EVELYN. He never had a heart problem in his life before then.

ROGER. That you were aware of. But who knows? He ate meat every night, didn't exercise, he was under a ton of stress trying to keep the business open –

EVELYN. You can explain it any way you want, but I know what he died from. The whole last year, he wasn't the same man.

CAROL. It was because of Grandpa, not because of you.

EVELYN. I should have been more tolerant. Grandpa was old. He was sick.

CAROL. And that gave him the right to treat you like shit? Let's face it, he was a selfish son-of-a-bitch.

EVELYN. Please, he was still your grandfather…

CAROL. He was a miserable man, Ma. You want to hear something you didn't know? I'm the one who supplied him with cigars.

EVELYN. You?

CAROL. He gave me a nickel a cigar. He told me they didn't hurt his health, that you were just using that as an excuse, because you didn't like the way they stunk up the house.

ROGER. And you believed him?

CAROL. I was ten years old. Honest to God, up until just now, I never realized the position he put me in. I was giving cigars to a man who couldn't breathe.

(*to* **EVELYN**)

On top of which, he had me believing that you were this miserable shrew who was denying him the only pleasure he had left in his life.

EVELYN. Why didn't you tell me?

CAROL. He made me swear not to. And I was petrified of him.

EVELYN. I wish I had known that. What a horrible thing, manipulating his own grandchild.

(*to* **ROGER**)

Did he ever do anything like that to you?

ROGER. No. Then again, I'm not even sure he knew my name. He used to call me, 'Hey, you.' When he wasn't calling me a stupid vantz. If we're being honest here, Mom, given the way he behaved, I'm amazed that you were willing to put him in such a nice place.

EVELYN. He was still my husband's father. And I really did believe he would get the care he needed there.

ROGER. You must have had to stretch yourself plenty thin to pay for it.

EVELYN. I didn't realize how thin. After your father died, I found out he had cashed in his life insurance policy because the business was doing even worse than he told me.

ROGER. Jesus.

CAROL. I didn't know he ever had life insurance.

EVELYN. We got it after you were born. He didn't think we needed it. But I said, 'God forbid, the unthinkable happens. We're protected.' Not exactly the way it worked out. He was gone and we had a hundred dollars in the bank.

ROGER. And that's when you went back to work?

EVELYN. It was July. There were no teaching jobs yet. So, the first thing I did was sell the store. Harry, who'd worked there all those years, gave me fifteen hundred dollars for it. It was probably worth half that, but I think he felt sorry for us.

ROGER. Everybody felt sorry for us. That's the thing I hated the most. We were "Poor Evelyn, and the kids.' I still remember Mrs. Miller from 3E taking Carol and me to Coney Island. Every two minutes she'd grab us and say, 'You poor things. What a tragedy.'

CAROL. Yeah, that made me feel better. And I'm still trying to figure out how she came to the conclusion that the best way to help us alleviate our grief was to stick us in the front car of the Cyclone.

ROGER. By ourselves.

EVELYN. My head wasn't clear then. She offered to take you, I didn't think to tell her that motion sickness runs in the family.

CAROL. I can't believe you've been sitting on all this guilt for so long. Maybe if you'd shared it with us, we could have helped you.

EVELYN. I didn't want to burden you. You were children.

CAROL. Ma, we haven't been children for thirty years. This is what family is for, to share things like this.

EVELYN. What can I tell you? Since your father died, I've been doing everything on my own. I was an independent woman when nobody was fighting to be one. So now, going from independent to dependant...it's not so easy.

CAROL. Talking about how you feel has nothing to do with being dependant.

ROGER. It enables the listener to offer feedback and coping strategies.

(EVELYN and CAROL both stare at him.)

ROGER. I started therapy three months ago...As long as we're laying everything out on the table.

CAROL. You're kidding?

ROGER. It was Allison's idea. But the more I thought about it, the more it made sense to me.

EVELYN. Why do you need therapy?

ROGER. I've got problems like everybody else. Sometimes it helps to have a place to go and unload.

CAROL. When my marriage started to hit the rocks, Ira and I went to counseling. It didn't work. Of course, that had a lot to do with the fact that he was screwing my friend Robin.

EVELYN. *(to CAROL)* I knew you went to see a therapist, but...

(to ROGER)

You, I had no idea.

CAROL. How'd you know I went?

EVELYN. Lisa told me.

CAROL. She did? Then why didn't you say something?

EVELYN. I didn't want to intrude. I thought if you wanted me to know, you would have told me.

CAROL. But since you knew already, what was the point of keeping it to yourself?

(to ROGER)

Did you know, too?

ROGER. Uh...well...Are we still laying everything out on the table?

CAROL. Yes.

ROGER. I didn't know you and Ira went for marriage counseling, but I did know he was screwing Robin.

CAROL. What?! You knew? And you didn't fucking tell me?

ROGER. I didn't know while he was doing it, I found out after. And up until two minutes ago, I didn't know that you knew.

EVELYN. Why should he upset you more than necessary?

CAROL. But I already knew.

ROGER. I didn't know that you knew.

CAROL. This is unbelievable. Look at what we've been sitting on all this time. I mean, if the building thing hadn't come up – we all went through the same thing: you lost a husband, we lost a father...Now I understand why you reacted the way you did when you heard us talking about putting you in a nursing home. But, Ma, you're nothing like Grandpa.

ROGER. When it comes to difficult, you don't hold a candle to him.

CAROL. Not even close.

EVELYN. Yet. Who knows what kind of shape I'll be in ten years? If I live that long. It's not just the mental. It's the physical, too. I don't want to be a burden. One fall, one slip in the shower, and just like that, you can't take care of yourself. All of a sudden, you're pushing a walker with tennis balls on the bottom. It's not humiliating enough that you need the damn thing in the first place, they can't find something better than tennis balls?

CAROL. If you get to a point where you can't take care of yourself, you'll come live with me. And no tennis balls, I promise.

EVELYN. That should help you find a husband – 'We have to be quiet, my mother's sleeping in the next room.'

ROGER. So you'll live with me on Long Island.

EVELYN. I'm not moving to the country.

ROGER. Long Island is not the country.

EVELYN. This is my home. This is where I want to stay no matter what.

ROGER. Then you will. And if you get sick and need help, we'll bring people in. Around the clock if necessary.

EVELYN. That'll cost a fortune.

ROGER. I'll take care of it.

EVELYN. I don't want you to be under the same kind of pressure your father was.

ROGER. It's not a problem. I can afford whatever it costs.

EVELYN. You have your own family, I don't want you to use up all your savings.

ROGER. Don't worry. Allison would never let that happen.

(CAROL's cell phone rings and she answers it.)

CAROL. Hello? Oh, shit. I forgot. I'm sorry...Hold on a second.

(CAROL hands the phone to EVELYN.)

CAROL. Lisa wants to ask you something.

(EVELYN takes the phone from CAROL.)

EVELYN. Hello, Darling...I'm fine. How are you?...The lead? That's wonderful...Of course, I still have it. It's buried in a box in the closet. When do you need it by?...Oy. Okay, I'll find it and give it her before she comes home...

(EVELYN's confused about how to hang up the cell phone. She hands it to CAROL.)

EVELYN. She has the lead. My granddaughter the star.

ROGER. What's the play?

CAROL. 'Death of a Salesman.'

EVELYN. Isn't the lead in that Willy Loman?

CAROL. Usually. But in this version, it's Lilly Loman. It's an update with a feminist slant.

EVELYN. Crazy. Let me go find the coat for her. She wants the one with the fur collar. I think it's in a box in the...

(EVELYN crosses off.)

ROGER. Well, this has been one hell of a visit.

CAROL. You're not kidding. It's like a forty year-old time bomb just exploded. I've got all these images now, swirling around in my head. I remember we were at Rose's when we found out Daddy died.

ROGER. We were?

CAROL. Yeah. Sal was showing us a card trick. Then Mom walked in hysterical. There was a policeman with her... Rose grabbed her...Mom started screaming...

ROGER. I thought that happened here, in this apartment.

CAROL. No, we were across the hall.

ROGER. That part's a blur to me. But I do have a vivid memory of Aunt Sophie coming over and covering all the mirrors. And people sitting on those little benches. The whole thing scared the hell out of me...Strange, what sticks with you. Specific bits and pieces. And yet, when I try to remember Dad's voice, nothing.

CAROL. I can't hear it either. Sad. You ever think about what our lives would have been like if he hadn't died?

ROGER. Sometimes. You?

CAROL. I know he wouldn't have let me date half the shmucks I dated.

ROGER. You did lead quite a parade through the house.

CAROL. I had lousy self-esteem...You know, something you said yesterday really bothered me.

ROGER. What?

CAROL. That comment you made about me being bitter. That's really the way I come across?

ROGER. Well...

CAROL. We're being honest, remember?

ROGER. You know that stockbroker I fixed you up with a couple of months ago?

CAROL. Bob. I really liked him.

ROGER. The reason he never called you for a second date was because he thought you were a little...caustic.

CAROL. I knew it. I said to myself ten times that day, 'postpone the date.' I was a wreck. Ira had missed another alimony payment and I found out that I needed dental work that wasn't covered by my insurance. But there are so few nice guys out there.

ROGER. Don't give up so fast. We can try it again.

CAROL. You'll talk to Bob?

ROGER. Uh…I think the Bob ship has sailed. But I know other guys. I'll keep my eyes open.

CAROL. I really appreciate that…So, you're actually in therapy. Three months, huh?

ROGER. Yeah.

CAROL. Are you and Allison okay?

ROGER. We're basically solid. I mean, we've got our stuff. She wants to talk everything out. Me, I explode and head right for Best Buys. I got crap you wouldn't believe.

(EVELYN *enters with the coat. She hands it to* CAROL.)

EVELYN. I hope she doesn't mind the smell of moth balls.

ROGER. Wow. How old is that coat?

EVELYN. Let's put it this way, I wore it when your father and I went to see South Pacific with Mary Martin and Ezio Pinza.

ROGER. What year was that?

EVELYN. Please, I'm lucky I remember Mary Martin and Ezio Pinza. I've got stuff packed away, you wouldn't believe. One day, you'll come over we'll go through the boxes.

(*to* ROGER)

Somewhere I've got your father's old catcher's mitt, from when he played at Jefferson.

ROGER. Really? I'd love to have that.

EVELYN. (*to* CAROL) I'm sure there's plenty in there that you'll want, too.

CAROL. I may keep that coat.

EVELYN. Be my guest…Meanwhile, when I was looking for it, I was thinking about everything that transpired here the last couple of days. And, suddenly, the solution to the whole thing came to me. We should buy the apartment.

(ROGER *and* CAROL *look at each other.*)

ROGER. That's a good idea. I'm glad you thought of it.

EVELYN. Don't get smart with me.

CAROL. Ma, it's a big decision. Why don't you sleep on it?

EVELYN. I don't have to.

ROGER. Carol's right. Think about it overnight.

EVELYN. I made up my mind already. This way, whatever you lay out for my upkeep, you'll eventually make back when you sell. Plus, when I'm gone, there'll still be money for you to share.

CAROL. You'll probably outlive the both of us.

EVELYN. Bite your tongue. It's getting late. You should both go home.

CAROL. Are you sure you're okay?

EVELYN. I'm fine. Go home. I'll talk to you tomorrow. I love you both.

(**ROGER, CAROL** and **EVELYN** *hug, then* **ROGER** *and* **CAROL** *grab their coats and head for the door.*)

CAROL. Roger, give me a ride home.

ROGER. It's forty minutes out of my way.

CAROL. Big deal.

ROGER. I'll drop you off on Queens Boulevard. It's an express stop.

CAROL. You know what, forget the whole thing.

ROGER. All right. All right. I'll take you.

CAROL. Why didn't you just say that in the first place?

(**ROGER** *and* **CAROL** *exit.* **EVELYN** *crosses to the spot on the kitchen table where* **ABE** *smashed his cane. She runs her hand along the edge of the table and sighs. There's a knock at the door and* **ROSE** *enters.*)

ROSE. Hi.

EVELYN. Hello.

ROSE. I just heard Carol and Roger leave.

EVELYN. What do you keep a chair outside my door?

ROSE. I was waiting. So what happened?

EVELYN. I told them everything. About Benny, about Abe.

ROSE. Good. I'm glad you finally got it all off your chest. What did they say?

EVELYN. They were very understanding. We talked, we worked some things out. It brought us a little closer. Which is important. Because rumor has it, my best friend is moving.

ROSE. I wanted to tell you myself. I just didn't know how.

EVELYN. What's the big secret? You're an old woman, you got one daughter, you want to be with her.

ROSE. It's not just that. Evelyn, I'm sick. My doctor says I need dialysis.

EVELYN. What?

ROSE. Dialysis.

EVELYN. I heard the word –

ROSE. That's why I'm moving to Connie. She doesn't want me to go through it alone...without her there to help me.

EVELYN. Your kidneys suddenly got so much worse?

ROSE. It's not that sudden. The doctor's been saying for a while that it was inevitable. But I didn't want to deal with it, so I put it out of my mind. Then, last Wednesday, I went for a checkup and, when he got the results back, he said it was time. He wants me to start in the next couple of weeks.

EVELYN. Oh, Rose...

ROSE. I'm going to wait until I get to Connie's.

EVELYN. How long before you go?

ROSE. The doctor says I could live for years.

EVELYN. How long before you go to California?

ROSE. Oh. I'm leaving on the thirtieth.

EVELYN. Rose. Rose. What am I going to do without you?

ROSE. I don't know what I'm going to do without you either. We've been like sisters since the day you moved in here. I had just had Connie and you were busting at the seams with Carol. We were such nervous mothers.

EVELYN. It was like the blind leading the blind.

ROSE. What did we have? There were no books, no classes, no videos.

EVELYN. Back then a nanny was just a goat.

ROSE. And Sal, God bless him, he was no help. He stuck Connie once with a diaper pin and that was the end of it. He never changed her again.

EVELYN. Benny didn't mind changing a diaper. He used to brag that he got his technique from wrapping lamp chops.

ROSE. They were some pair, those two, with their stairway races – grown men, arguing about who got to the bottom first.

EVELYN. I can still picture them in front of the building, playing salugi with Roger. And me yelling out the window, 'watch out for the cars'.

ROSE. So, the kids told me you were talking about buying the apartment.

EVELYN. I wasn't going to do it, but after we all discussed it, I think it's a good idea. Roger's going to work the whole thing out with the financing and the paperwork. It's unbelievable. Two hundred and fifty thousand dollars to own a little piece of the Nathan Hale Apartments. 'My only regret is...

ROSE AND EVELYN. ...that I have but one elevator to give to my tenants.'

ROSE. Fifty years. Where did the time go?

EVELYN. I don't know. You were my rock.

ROSE. It takes a lot out of you, dialysis. Evelyn, I'm scared.

EVELYN. You'll handle it. Aside from your kidneys, you're not in such terrible shape.

ROSE. Right. I've got an artificial valve, a pacemaker, and a stent. Before my last surgery, they asked me, if something should go wrong, do I want to donate my body parts. I said, 'the only thing my parts are good for is to rebuild a helicopter.'

(EVELYN *laughs.*)

EVELYN. You may not be as healthy as some people, but you have an iron will.

ROSE. That I do.

ROSE. You still have that old bottle of Scotch laying around?

EVELYN. Yes. But you're not supposed to drink.

ROSE. One's not going to kill me.

EVELYN. I'll make it a small one.

(**EVELYN** *takes an old bottle of Scotch from the back of the cabinet. During the following she gets two glasses and pours them each a shot.*)

ROSE. They make advances in medicine and look what happens. On, the one hand, I get the benefit. With heart problems like mine, twenty years ago, I would have been dead and buried already. Instead, I lived to see my grandchildren, this, that and other thing. On the other hand, they've kept me alive so long, I could end up with every medical condition in the book.

EVELYN. Our children will have it easier. They're more aware and they already take better care of themselves.

ROSE. Connie started on medication for osteoporosis a couple of years ago.

EVELYN. Carol's on it now, too. Osteoporosis runs in our family. I was five foot five when I moved in this building. Soon I'll be able to fit in your pocket.

ROSE. I'll tell you one good thing about California. No snow, no ice. I know two people who slipped and fell this winter and broke their hips.

EVELYN. That's the big one. Somebody should design a line of clothing for seniors made out of bubble wrap. They'd make a fortune.

ROSE. It's a good idea. Well, at least we still have all our marbles.

EVELYN. We're lucky. Although some days I think a little dementia wouldn't be such a bad thing, if I could pick what to forget.

ROSE. I never wanted to think of this day. When one of us would leave the building.

EVELYN. Me either. But let's not get carried away. It's not like we're never going to see each other again. I'll come and visit.

ROSE. When was the last time you got on a plane?

EVELYN. Years ago. But since then, I haven't had a good reason. Now I have one.

ROSE. You'll really come?

EVELYN. Try to keep me away. You'll get settled, I'll be on the first plane out with a box of cannolis from Ferrara's.

ROSE. Don't wait too long. Because you never know.

EVELYN. Stop that kind of talk right now. You're going to be okay. You've got Connie there, you've got your faith. God is going to look after you.

ROSE. I thought you didn't believe in God.

EVELYN. For you, I'm making an exception.

ROSE. It stinks, getting old.

EVELYN. I'll drink to that.

(They pick up their glasses.)

ROSE. Salud.

EVELYN. L'chaim.

(They click glasses and down the shots.)

The End

PROP LIST

ACT ONE
SCENE ONE

Sunday New York Times
Microwave
Coffee pot
Coffee cups
Dinner plates
Drinking glasses
Silverware
Coffee
Tea bags
Creamer
Sugar bowl
Container of milk
Twenty dollar bill
Reading glasses
Cheesecake
Napkin holder that holds some letters

SCENE THREE
Dinner plates
Sliced turkey
Sliced cheddar cheese
Half a rye bread
Jar of deli mustard
Old savings bankbook
Cordless phone

ACT TWO
SCENE TWO

Two cell phones
Container of Milk
Two raw potatoes
Potato Peeler
Small bouquet of flowers
Cane
1950's ladies coat with fur collar
Bottle of Scotch
Two small glasses

SET DESIGN

ARCH DOORWAY

Breinigsville, PA USA
16 December 2010
251635BV00005B/10/P